What Do You Think About?

What Do You Think About?

Poems That Keep You Thinking

S T Kimbrough, Jr.

Foreword by Charles Amjad-Ali

RESOURCE *Publications* · Eugene, Oregon

WHAT DO YOU THINK ABOUT?
Poems That Keep You Thinking

Resource Publications
An Imprint of Wipf and Stock Publishers
199 W. 8th Ave., Suite 3
Eugene, OR 97401

www.wipfandstock.com

PAPERBACK ISBN: 978-1-6667-4494-1
HARDCOVER ISBN: 978-1-6667-4495-8
EBOOK ISBN: 978-1-6667-4496-5

May 31, 2022 4:01 PM

CONTENTS

Foreword by Charles Amjad-Ali   *vi*

Introduction   *xii*

SECTION 1   WHAT DO YOU THINK ABOUT YOURSELF?

  1. Soul-Composure   3

  2. Self-Denial   4

  3. Self-Effacement   5

  4. Self-Pity   6

  5. Self-Satisfied   7

  6. We Are Not Made for Self Alone   8

  7. What Will I Be?   9

  8. Being Alone   10

  9. We Know What We Are   11

10. You and I   12

11. Mirrors of the Soul   13

12. Know Thyself?   14

13. Inside and Out   15

14. Crying and Weeping   16

15. The Subconscious   17

SECTION 2   WHAT DO YOU THINK ABOUT TIME?

16. Time 1   21

17. Time 2   22

18. It's Time   23

19. The In-Between   24

20. Wasting Time   25

21. From Evening to Morn   26

22. Family Time   27

23. Making Family Music   28

24. Today Will Soon Be Yesterday   30

25. What a Day!   31

26. Then and Now   32

27. Backward—Forward   33

28. A Future from Our Past   34

SECTION 3   **WHAT DO YOU THINK OF WHAT YOU THINK?**

29. To Think   37

30. The Power of Thoughts   38

31. The Wonder of Thoughts   39

32. Sober Thoughts   40

33. Conscience   41

34. The Senses   42

35. Three Gifts   43

36. The Link   44

37. Knowledge Versus Ignorance   45

38. Learn Kindness   46

39. Kindness, A Frame of Mind   47

40. Fortune   48

41. Reality 1   49

SECTION 4   **WHAT DO YOU THINK REALLY MATTERS?**

42. Peace and Quiet   53

43. Arrogance   54

44. Pessimism?   55

45. Ambiguity 1   56

46. Ambiguity 2   57

47. Reality 2   58

48. Daily Greetings   59

49. Sadness and Joy   60

50. What Matters   61

51. Life and Love   62

52. Life and Death   63

53. Poetry   64

54. I Cannot Be Human Alone   65

55. Humility   66

56. Hopeless?   67

57. Goodness   68

Section 5   What Do You Think Makes You Smile?

58. An Octogenarian Viewpoint   71

59. Blue   72

60. Cobblestones   73

61. Forget / Remember   74

62. Mama's Blouse   75

63. Melodrama   76

64. Ole Jack   77

65. Que sera sera?   78

66. Tea Time for Leo and Lou   79

67. The Sugar Cane Trust   80

68. Moonlit Railroad Tracks   82

69. This or That   83

70. Two Styles   84

71. You   85

72. Uncle Lane's Sugar Cane   86

73. Grandma and Grandpa's House   87

74. Poor Mumford   88

SECTION 6   WHAT DO YOU THINK OF LOVE?

75. What Is Love?   91

76. A Thought of Love   92

77. Child Love   93

78. Family Love   94

79. In Love   95

80. Love and Trust   96

81. Love   97

82. Love's Abode   98

83. More Than Life   99

84. Oh, For a Love Like Yours!   100

85. Singing Eyes   101

86. The Greatest Power   102

87. The Joy of Senses   103

88. They Well Combine   104

89. To Love   105

90. The Day Begins   106

91. Resistless Love   107

Bibliography   109

FOREWORD

S T KIMBROUGH, JR., has spent a lifetime working with the Old Testament—with a Ph.D. in Old Testament and Semitic Languages from Princeton Theological Seminary—and also a lifetime with ecclesial institutions. In addition to this, he is a highly accomplished operatic singer and was the baritone in the Bonn Opera Company in Germany when I, as a student, first met him in the 1970s. He has produced a large repertoire of music albums, everything from opera to hymns, etc. As he states, "I've sung opera, sung songs / around the world before great throngs." A constant throughout his long and varied career has been his love for, and deep commitment to, the Wesleyan tradition, especially its hymnody and lyrics, which have profoundly influenced him, and about which he has written extensively. Thus Hebrew Bible, music, lyrics and the poetic expressions in them, and indeed theology, have been the moving force in his long gifted life.

The passing in 2016 of Sarah, S T's much beloved wife and his anchor and beacon, has made him think anew on all the different aspects of his life and experiences. He has had a rebirth of these different vocations, expressing them poetically, shifting the cognitive processes and faith expressions through metaphor and rhyme. He has put together ten wonderful volumes of poetry over these years. Sarah has clearly been the muse and spirit which has guided him, as this vocational shift began with her passing away. She was obviously the core inspiration behind his first book of poetry, dealing with death, grief, healing, and renewal. S T has broadened his analogical imagination and poetic expression to deal with deep existential concerns: peace and justice in the Middle East; deep concern for nature and the environment; even the present ubiquitous, and dare I say omnipresent, Coronavirus and how in its initial phase it caused grief and death and its sword of Damocles-like presence over all our collective heads and the ideological fights it has generated. He has also delved into the issues of wrestling with Christian faith, truth, doubt, and certitudes.

This volume, *What Do You Think About? Poems That Keep You Thinking*, addresses many of these issues afresh, but now within the context of a reflective life which cannot be reduced to some non-thinking banality: "To think is an auspicious gift to everyone in humankind. Don't let your thoughts then go adrift, but nurture them within your mind." S T is, however, not necessarily viewing this reflective process simply through the lens of Hannah Arendt's *The Life of the Mind*, or Martin Heidegger's, *Discourse on Thinking*,[1] but is closer to René Descartes' meditations, i.e., *cogito ergo sum*,[2] "I think, therefore I am." S T, however, balances this with "I am (with all the nurture), therefore I think;" he thus poses the reflective life in a deep dialectic between thinking and being in our present times, when the art of thinking is moving towards extinction, as is the art of truth telling. He therefore invokes both these aspects of reflective life. The invocation to truth telling is a highly critical vocation and clearly has political and moral implications and a quest for virtue which are in short demand and are based on the biblical imperative of knowing the truth and of knowledge freeing us (John 8:32). "Above all, we were taught to think," he writes: "Honesty, Truth, Respect." All language acquires critical importance in this context, which grounds our acts of communication and interlocution in these truths and virtues: Is it about power or ethics? power or justice? power or virtue? etc.

> What raises thoughts today to heights
>   of meaning everyone should know?
> Perhaps if they broach human rights,
>   they'll shatter thoughts of old Jim Crow?
>
>   . . .
>
> Our thoughts have power to create
>   a different world in which to live.
> Yet, progress they can obviate
>   when we refuse them power to give.

1. Arendt, *The Life of the Mind*; and Heidegger, *Discourse on Thinking*.

2. Descartes, *Discourse on the Method of Rightly Conducting One's Reason and of Seeking Truth in the Sciences*.

We should therefore not be led astray by sophistries randomly uttered for the maintenance of power, but be guided by a reflective life dealing with the reality and facts around us in our lives.

S T brings his different themes together with compassion, empathy, and wisdom, and even nostalgia, which shines through each of the poems in this volume. When he asks us to be responsible agents, he is not assuming an isolated individual of the Hobbsian (total fallen) humanity and emphatic individuality (which is nasty, brutish, and short), but with the vocational concerns of a redeemed humanity in the Cross. This makes the individual deeply connected with and committed to be with others, nurtured by and nurturing them, and helped by and helping them navigate the complexities of life, thus enlarging the circle of God's grace and compassion, critical for the understanding of the incarnation and the cross. Citing Gregory of Nazianzus he exhorts us,

> With Gregory, resist greed's claim
>   that we should live for self alone.
> Let good of others be our aim;
>   gross selfishness learn to disown.

This compassion plays a foundational role in S T's operatic poetic imagination and helps us navigate difficult and complex issues through the use of metaphor. In doing so his reflective process negates the absurdity of classical Hobbesian flat prose used as a methodological paradigm, viz:

> "*Causes of absurdity:* . . . the use of metaphors, tropes, and other rhetorical figures, instead of word proper. For though it be lawful to say, for example, in common speech, *the way goeth, or leadeth hither, or thither; the proverb says this or that*, whereas way cannot go, nor proverb speak; yet in reckoning, and seeking truth, such speeches are not to be admitted."[3]

What a sad and banal way of approaching life! Poetic and metaphoric imaginations have an innate way of opening and "letting come forth" worlds in the configuration of words and metaphors and synecdoches and similes and how they are laid out. This book is indeed a symphony of these instruments, melodies, and lyrics.[4]

In this, S T's poetry resonates with Heidegger's deep commitment to be *Sorge* and *besorgen*—to be caring. To be human is to be caring. That

---

3. Hobbes, *Leviathan, or the Matter, Form, and Power of a Commonwealth*, 43–44.

4. Heidegger, *Poetry, Language, Thought*.

caring for each other and the world is a thread that runs throughout this volume of poetry. S T's poems are a deep reflection and thinking on these issues and guiding us to navigate new terrain and new and creative language and to be open to the revealing of and the letting come forth of the muse.

It forces us to reflect on the biblical command to reason together and invite others to share in this reasoning. S T shows us that songs, music, and poetry are a profound way of grasping God's word ever anew and that this muse impacts us, so we are, to use a German word, *gebildet*, and we experience *Bildung*. Both these words have a reference to *Bild* and refer to the *imago*, the image in which we were created, i.e., the image of God (*imago dei*) (Genesis 1:27). The contemporary use of *Bildung* minimizes it simply as formal education, forgetting its classic understanding based on the mysticism which viewed education as an expanding and enhancing of the image of God dwelling in us, and then we are educated for proper interactions with life, God, nature, and our neighbors. That is what we have to reason together, or to quote Isaiah "Come now, let us reason/argue it out, says the Lord" which has clear salvific implication because "though your sins are like scarlet, they shall be like snow; though they are red like crimson, they shall become like wool" (Isaiah 1:18 NRSV). So in this collection of poetries both here and in the previous collections, S T always combines aesthetics (*aesthesis*), with ethics and with the art of *eudaemonia* (inadequately thought to be *happiness* (?) even in our Declaration of Independence), which is about human flourishing or expanding the image of God in us, and that is *Bildung*.

> Life, liberty, and happiness,
> these rights belong to all,
> yet millions know but emptiness,
> democracy's downfall.

In the context of these poems, it is interesting to remember that Greek language and philosophy define the act of making, engendering, and creating in two distinct words/concepts. Both these words have a place in the English language in their original form and at least partially convey their original Greek meaning and philosophical nuances. The first of these is *techne* (from which we get our words "technology," "technique," etc.). Generally, philosophically *techne* refers to the process of "making or doing," and is often used to distinguish it from the second word we will consider, namely *poiesis*—art. *Poiesis* etymologically means "the act or process of making," but this activity entails a person bringing something into being that did not exist in that form before. While *techne* means making more actively, i.e., something that is worked upon, *poiesis* entails more passive activities in this making and entails helping something to come from and express its original sources. It's like Michelangelo, who claimed that he was not *sculpting* David from any block of marble, but was actually involved in the process of releasing David from a particular block of marble, which he searched for and which (according to him) already contained David. So he acts as midwife to the birth of David. Similarly, these poems are muses that are being given form and each an expression of that which is released for human compassion and well-being.

S T in his poems has taken us in a slight loop away from the laboratory of scientific and technical certitude to a faith language and poetry which has tensions and doubts, and generates new thoughts and imagination. Through poetry he guides us to different ways we can take in our journeys, paths we can travel, where unexpected light shines through the dark forests and in that moment of light we have moments of belief, even if we began the journey in darkness, doubt, disbelief, and anxiety.[5] Poetry is as precise in its areas of reflection as natural scientific language, because it deals with a completely different set of complexities, viz., the difference between *knowing* and *explaining*. While the latter has been classically defined as the way we approach natural sciences and their explanatory character (i.e., *Erklärung*); understanding (i.e., *Verstehen*) entails a different set of knowledge, which demands to *stand under*—not in unquestionable certitude, but rather it requires and utilizes metaphors, analogies, similes, etc., to bring to light the new, and forces us to think differently. Paul Ricouer even argues that metaphors are language-generating.[6] In our contemporary world, with the dogmatic assertions and total acceptance of natural scientific explanation as being of the highest value, this poetic approach of understanding is not cognitively accommodated, and neither is the new that is revealed through it, thus anathematizing poetic assertions and viewing the knowledge gained as almost heretical or at best simply romantic.

In medieval philosophy the human had a dual intellectual agency as having both active intellect (*intellectus agens*) and passive or potential intellect (*intellectus possibilis*). So we received God's creation passively (for example, birds) and through our active intellect differentiated these birds and named them (for example, sparrow, owl, etc.). This was indeed the first of

5. Heidegger, *Off the Beaten Track*.
6. Ricouer, *Interpretation Theory*, esp. 5.

God's imperatives on humans: "every animal of the field and every bird of the air, [God] brought them to the man to see what he would call them; and whatever the man called every living creature, that was its name" (Genesis 2:19 NRSV). In this process Human became co-creator with God, according to Thomas Aquinas, and brought into being that which did not exist before. There was a combination of all these different aspects of knowledge, and that is the work of art and poetry, which S T has so beautifully displayed in his meditations on the art of thinking and caring.

> The good in knowledge to be found
>   is goodness to be shared.
> Though ignorance may still abound,
>   choose knowledge, uncompared.

Rev. Charles Amjad-Ali, Ph.D., Th.D.
The Martin Luther King, Jr.,
Prof. of Justice and Christian Community (Emeritus)
Director of Islamic Studies (Emeritus)
Luther Seminary, St. Paul, MN
The Desmond Tutu Prof. of Ecumenical Theology
and Social Transformation in Africa (Emeritus)
University of Western Cape
Cape Town, South Africa

Introduction

THE POWERFUL PLAY *Inherit the Wind* by Jerome Lawrence and Robert E. Lee is a theatrical portrayal, though written in a historical-fiction style, of the famous Scopes trial that took place during July 1925 in Dayton, Tennessee, which addressed the issue of the right to teach the theory of evolution in public schools. In the play there are ongoing insightful exchanges between the lawyer for the defense, Henry Drummond, who represents the historical trial lawyer Clarence Darrow, and Matthew Harrison Brady, who was the chief counsel opposed to the theory of evolution and who represented the historical figure of William Jennings Bryan. The play is filled with Brady's vigorous efforts to defend an inerrant view of the Bible, and what he perceives to be the Bible's accurate description of creation.

In questioning Brady regarding the biblical account of creation Drummond asks

> DRUMMOND: That first day. Was it a twenty-four-hour day?
> BRADY: The Bible says it was a day.
> DRUMMOND: There wasn't any sun. How do you know how long it was?
> BRADY: The Bible says it was a day.
> DRUMMOND: A normal day, a literal day, a twenty-four-hour day?
> BRADY: I don't know.
> DRUMMOND: What do you think?
> BRADY: I do not think about things that . . . I do not think about.[7]

This book of poems is titled "What Do You Think About? Poems That Keep You Thinking." It is desperately important to think about the things that we tend to push aside, questions and issues that it is easier to avoid. Each of the six sections of poems is prefaced with a question: What do you think about yourself? What do you think about time? What do you think

---

7. Lawrence and Lee, *Inherit the Wind*, 69.

of what you think? What do you think really matters? What do you think makes you smile? What do you think of love?

Many of the poems share the wisdom of my parents which they knowingly or unknowingly imparted to me while growing up in a loving household with two sisters. From both my parents and my sisters I learned much of what surfaces in these poems. *Above all, we were taught to think.* While my parents did not quote the Roman poet Horace's *Sapere aude* (Dare to know, or dare to think/to be wise), they certainly lived by this affirmation. They knew that thinking is not easy, and they did not want us to grow up intellectually bankrupt. Hence to avoid thinking was not an option, as easy as that is for almost everyone.

I learned early on that to be tolerant of differences in thinking was not always easy but necessary. Above all, to be a "caregiving thinker"[8] required patience, persistence, and risk. Furthermore, "What is needed for the life of thinking is *hope*: hope of knowing more, understanding more, *being* more than we currently are."[9] Hope is a recurrent theme in many of the poems found here.

> What we are we think that we know,
>   but not what we may be.
> What's in between we can't forego;
>   the future we can't see.
>
>   . . .
>
> Try as we may, there is no way
>   clairvoyance to turn on.
> And yet we know that come what may,
>   *we'll hope for a new dawn.*[10]
>
> Expect the best and hope will guide
>   your acts, emotions, and your thought.
> Then pessimism cannot hide
>   behind "to hope is all for naught."[11]

"Honesty, Truth, Respect" were underlying principles of our lives without their having to be so labeled. While our parents instilled in us a sense of honest pride, it was never allowed to express itself in "Arrogance."

8. See Jacobs, *How to Think.*

9. Ibid., 151.

10. See poem #9. Italics added for emphasis.

11. See poem #44.

We understood that "Love Is Why" we existed as a family, and we experienced early on both "Sadness and Joy." No doubt, my parents and sisters are one of the primary reasons that the theme of "Love" appears in the poems of Section 6. Most of the subjects addressed in these poems I was encouraged to think about.

As I grew to an adult, I learned well the meaning of a Greek proverb, which my mother put into cross-stitch for me and had framed. It still hangs in my study and says: "Life is not worth living unless all of one's talents are pursued along lines leading to excellence." While this is a foreboding proverb to face as a youngster, it has helped me through the years to understand the difference between "Self-Effacement," "Self-Pity," and being "Self-Satisfied." I certainly learned to avoid "Wasting Time" and to value the importance of a "Conscience." However, self-preoccupation can prevent thinking with others in community and moving from a concept of "others" to "neighbors."

Did I think beyond the present and myself in its context? Did I think about the future? Of course, I did and still do. That's why such poems as "Today Will Be Yesterday," "From Evening to Morn," "Life and Death," and "Life and Love," are found here.

My parents, Dorothy and S T, were blessed with a marvelous sense of humor. My father especially seemed to have an endless repertory of jokes and funny stories. I remember a book he used to read to me when I was a young boy, which began with the lines, "There was a funny little man, in a funny little house, on a funny little road." By the time he had come to the end of the first page, he was usually laughing so much, he could scarcely continue. Perhaps it is not surprising that he died in the midst of telling a joke to a practical nurse employed by the hospital to which he had been admitted. I was not present at the time of his passing, which was quite sudden. However, when I arrived at the hospital, the practical nurse apologized but wanted to know if I could finish the funny story my father was telling when he died. My father had not gotten to the punch line or climax before expiring. That may seem macabre to some but not to me, for in his billfold when he died I found a grocery store receipt on which two Bible references were written: Psalm 2:4 (KJV), "God sits in the heavens and laughs." Beside this reference he had written, "And we know why." Below these words was the reference of Joel 2:28 (KJV), "And it shall come to pass afterward, that I will pour out my spirit upon all flesh; and your sons and your daughters shall prophesy, your old men shall dream dreams, your young men shall see visions." Whether or not my father expressed his dreams in words, I feel certain that he was a constant dreamer. It seems that even immediately prior to his death, he was thinking about the importance of laughter and dreams.

My mother was also filled with quick wit. On her ninety-second birthday, I phoned to wish her a happy birthday, and said, "How are you doing, Mother?" She replied, "Oh son, the wrinkles don't bother me. It's all the sagging." Then she burst into laughter. At ninety-seven years of age on the very last Christmas before her death, she still exhibited amazingly quick wit. She, I, and her great granddaughter, Hannah, were standing in a breezeway of the retirement home where she lived, waiting for Hannah's father, my son Timothy, to drive his car to that area so that we could ride with him. My mother suddenly asked, "Hannah, what grade are you in?" Hannah replied, "The seventh. What about you, Mama K?" (the affectionate name her grandchildren called her). Mother replied, "Oh, I've already quit-uated." Hannah burst into laughter, as did I. The cleverness of combining "quit" with part of the word "graduated" still amuses me. What amazingly quick wit she had!

I have never forgotten what my mother said to me when I went out on my first date with a young girl in high school. "Son, just remember what it says on the top of the Kraft mayonnaise jar." She said nothing more. Unknown to me, she was pressing me to think, to think about the meaning of relationships. I had no idea what she had in mind, but she knew I would look in the refrigerator where a jar of mayonnaise was kept. Before leaving on my date, I opened the door of the refrigerator to see what was written there. It said, "Keep cool but do not freeze." In some ways I think this was some of my mother's best advice for life itself, and which she no doubt knew I would think about for years to come.

Given the importance of my parents' influence, it is not surprising that some of my poems have a rather homespun, humorous quality about them. My parents taught me to laugh, for which I am forever grateful, as my poem "An Octogenarian Viewpoint" indicates. Perhaps laughter and humor are reasons why I delight in word play in such poems as, "Forget / Remember," "You," and "This or That."

I nowhere suggest that my thoughts are definitive for others. They are my personal thoughts which emerged from a loving home with a joyous Christian ethos where I was taught to think. Please take them for what they are: my personal reflections. I do suggest, however, that appreciating life as it is around us and those who surround us, is one of the most vital aspects of being a fulfilled human being. Nevertheless, I am aware that not everyone has a joyous childhood in a loving family. If my experiences help to give others insight into the values of thinking about what we do and don't think about, then sharing these poems will have been worthwhile. I share T. S. Eliot's view expressed in "Four Quartets" (1943), "Whatever you think, be sure it is what you think."

Section 1

What Do You Think About Yourself?

1. SOUL-COMPOSURE

A soul that contemplates the day
    in quiet and repose,
may troubles of the self allay,
    perhaps the soul compose—

compose the inner self with calm,
    the outer self as well.
Repose and quiet are the balm
    anxieties can quell.

But there's a calm each one should seek,
    no troubles will address.
It's peace without a low or peak;
    it's peace that knows no stress.

You rise, go forth, in peace retire,
    the soul has found a peace
that wrestles not with forces dire;
    the soul seeks not release.

Is possible such calm estate
    without distress or frets?
Indeed, it's not a stroke of fate.
    The problem—one forgets.

2. SELF-DENIAL

One winter morn, December first,
    I woke with quite a start.
The sunlight through my windows burst,
    its rays swift as a dart.

My eyelids blinked, slowly I tried
    to sunlight to adjust.
Beneath the covers tried to hide,
    but, no, get up I must.

My mother called, "It's time to rise,
    Today's our fasting day."
I wondered, "Is that really wise?"
    I knew not what to say.

Then I recalled at each year's end
    we fast that we may give
the money we for food would spend,
    that hungering folks may live.

How wise for me, a boy, to learn:
    "I must myself deny!"
Or never would I grasp, discern
    of hunger millions die.

3. Self-Effacement

There's little that I do not share,
    at least, somehow that's what I think.
But when I see a cupboard bare
    and someone's life lived on the brink,

the brink of hunger and despair,
    I see my cupboards are all full.
Is not my plenty my own snare,
    and does my conscience measure null?

How can I know I've done my part?
    How can I know I've done enough?
Yes, ask I must: Did I ev'n start?
    An honest answer's truly tough.

I think quite highly of myself,
    though my convictions, actions clash.
To put convictions on the shelf
    puts me myself right on the brink,

the brink of conflict and despair.
    If I have food, give none away,
I've shown once more I do not care;
    I've held the poor, hungry at bay.

4. SELF-PITY

Self-pity is a strange self-view.
You tell yourself, "I wish I knew
why I can't be more confident.
Alas, my state seems permanent.
What's more, my state's futility
and lacking in humility."
Self-pity's not humility;
its absence *is* futility.
If you will try humble to be,
perhaps self-pity then will flee.

5. SELF-SATISFIED

If I would be self-safisfied,
it must with diligence be tried.
Self-satisfied—can it be wrong?
Self-satisfied for all life long?
Self-satisfied can go amiss,
if others' feelings we dismiss.
Self-satisfied, self-centered's not,
but often in its trap we're caught.

Gregory of Nazianzus: "We are not made for ourselves alone;
we are made for the good of all our fellow creatures."

6. WE ARE NOT MADE FOR SELF ALONE

We are not made for self alone;
    we're made for good of all.
I fear that this is not well known,
    for greed's hard to forestall.

Of mutual caring there's a lack—
    to think of others first.
Such caring stands under attack:
    greed has an endless thirst.

Greed claims that for yourself you're made,
    for others need not care.
By others you need not be swayed,
    only of self aware.

With Gregory, resist greed's claim
    that we should live for self alone.
Let good of others be our aim;
    gross selfishness learn to disown.

7. WHAT WILL I BE?

I sat beneath a large oak tree,
    when I was only ten
and thought and thought what will I be
    when grown like other men.

When I was only sixteen years,
    I thought, I'll be a priest,
help others through their joys and tears,
    a worthwhile life at least.

At young nineteen I fell in love,
    love was my only thought.
Its ecstasy was far above
    all else; all else was naught.

With marriage came our own first son,
    what joy embraced my soul.
And family life had now begun,
    I in the father's role.

And then another boy was born;
    loved filled me more and more.
I never shall forget the morn
    the smile at birth he wore.

My true vocation now I knew:
    to love my family.
No matter what for pay I'd do,
    a lover I would be.

8. BEING ALONE

What does it mean to be alone?
    No one is there beside?
It means so much that is unknown.
    Who will meaning decide?

Does it mean only you are there
    and absence is the key?
Alone means absence of a pair,
    a partner one can't see?

With others one can be alone,
    ev'n in a boisterous crowd.
Aloneness everyone can own;
    we're all with it endowed.

Though absent one can still be there
    in thought, in love's strong tie.
The question is: Will we then dare
    sense presence though one die?

William Shakespeare: "We know what we are,
but know not what we may be."

9. WE KNOW WHAT WE ARE

What we are we think that we know,
    but not what we may be.
What's in between we can't forego;
    the future we can't see.

But oh, we plan and try so hard
    to know what is to be.
That's why we're often on our guard
    to see what we can see.

Try as we may, there is no way
    clairvoyance to turn on.
And yet we know that come what may,
    we'll hope for a new dawn.

10. You and I

The difference twixt you and me
    is I am I and you are you.
I wonder if we willingly
    think this is how that things should be.

Do I want you to be like me
    and you want me to be like you?
This is a problem we should see,
    for this is many people's view.

But I don't want to be like you,
    and you don't want to be like me.
And it's okay to have this view,
    and on this point we should agree.

I must respect your different views,
    as long as they will harm no one.
This is the path we all must choose;
    we must not one another shun!

11. Mirrors of the Soul

If minds are mirrors of the soul,
    what does one see reflected there?
Are images there that console
    since one is bold enough to share?
Does one see images of greed
    and images of self-concern,
if one ignores all others' need
    and is morose and taciturn?

One needs new images of good
    that come from showing that one cares
and acting as one knows one should,
    and burdens of another bears.
If one so acts, the soul reflects
    new images deep in the soul;
new images that won't perplex
    but make a selfish spirit whole.

12. KNOW THYSELF?

It seems that anger's grasped the earth
    in clutches of mistrust and hate.
Each moment opposition's birth
    promotes new evil we await.

Some politicians truth deny
    and govern but with words of war.
Dictators reason dare defy
    and goodness, kindness both ignore.

A season of distrust, despair,
    amid pandemic's lethal course,
is fostered by those who don't care—
    false information they enforce.

Whence disappeared life's sanctity?
    Is neighborliness gone for good?
Is lost for good veracity?
    And have we lost all personhood?

Did Socrates the Grecian art
    of "know thyself" conceive in vain?
Not if we look into the heart
    and are inspired to be humane!

"Who looks outside, dreams; who looks inside, wakes." Carl Jung

13. Inside and Out

To look outside means that we dream,
    to look inside means that we wake.
Outside are things not what they seem?
    Inside we do a double take.
A double take means we look twice,
    so inwardly our minds can see
that shallowness cannot suffice,
    suffice for thought-reality.

O yes, I dream, as it should be,
    but *only* dreams lead me astray,
if they make me an absentee
    from truth and what is real each day.
To waken as I look inside
    indeed is such a sharp contrast
to outside dreams that turn aside
    reality in ways that last.

But I would have inside and out;
    yes, I would dream and I would wake
to know myself without a doubt
    and know myself for my own sake.
It could just be that I will learn
    to wed dreams with reality.
Then shallow dreams I'll learn to spurn,
    and what is real I'll wake to see.

14. Crying and Weeping

Must I emotions quiet keep?
I sometimes cry, I sometimes weep.
I cry in joy, I cry in grief,
to cry and cry oft brings relief.
At dawn I cry, at night I cry;
sometimes I cry, I don't know why.
If I should cry, do I then weep?
Has it a nuance that's more deep?
One reads in Scripture "Jesus wept."
Should this translation then be kept,
instead of reading "Jesus cried"?
The pathos cannot be denied.
To weep stresses a depth within,
and crying's close, but not its twin.

15. THE SUBCONSCIOUS

Beneath the surface struggles reign,
beneath the surface struggles strain.
They strain between evil and good;
they ask, do we act as we should?
Beneath the surface we know not,
if we've remembered or forgot.
Subconsciously the mind's at work;
subconsciously strange thoughts may lurk.
How can our best thoughts come to be
the roots of our identity?
If we seek truth and honesty,
will our subconscious thoughts agree?
The chance is very strong they will;
truth, honesty will seek no ill.

Section 2

What Do You Think About Time?

16. TIME 1

Of time, is there enough to live?
    No one can this foresee.
Of time, is there enough to give
    of love which is the key?

Of time, we live and speculate
    that we may have enough.
Of time, we cannot calculate;
    it may our hopes rebuff.

Of time, we have the time to think,
    but will we use it well?
Our time with patience we should link,
    that thoughts on sense may dwell.

17. TIME 2

How can we *time* clearly define?
　　Just sixty minutes of an hour?
Three times a day that we may dine?
　　The daily hours that clocks devour?

Specific, yet illusive time,
　　of it we do not have enough.
It brings us sorrow, joy sublime;
　　its truth is often very tough.

How shall we then time calculate?
　　By deep reflection's silent art?
Hours twenty-four reiterate
　　until the cycle we re-start?

The repetition of the clock,
　　sometimes is only a routine;
and creativity we block
　　when we don't know what time it's been.

The time, more time, illusive time
　　slips quickly, speedily away.
This fact ignored and you'll say, "I'm
　　too careless and my life's caché.

18. It's Time

If we could truly turn back time,
    would it be worth the while,
to choose spring or another clime?
    Would our clothes be in style?

Romantic is the lovely thought
    that we might find the year
when nations wars no longer fought;
    the world was absent fear.

Is it then only just a dream
    to think we'll find a time
when peace, a universal theme,
    is in its worldwide prime?

There is no time that's without strife,
    no time of love's sole reign.
No time *each person* leads full life;
    no time devoid of pain.

No, time we never can turn back;
    we only have today,
and we can change the things we lack
    and find a smarter way.

By looking back our lives we'll make
    much better than before,
for we'll know what's *for all* at stake:
    each human soul cared for.

19. The In-Between

We're always living in between
    beginning and the end.
The space in time is always lean;
    we've scarcely time to spend.

Between our birth and death there's time,
    but we know not how long.
To some in life's rewarding prime
    death comes, though they seem strong.

The in-between reveals no plan,
    instructs not what to do,
but every woman, every man
    receives from time a clue.

The clue is this: you're born, you die,
    and in the in-between
the time you have's a truth or lie
    by what you are, have been.

20. Wasting Time

I find it hard to waste my time;
    sometimes I wish I could,
but I'd feel guilty and that I'm
    not doing what I should.

Some folk are masters of the task,
    for time they waste and waste.
Perhaps they never stop to ask,
    have I myself disgraced?

Disgraced by never seeking out
    my gifts and talents too,
for I was born without a doubt
    with things that I can do.

But these, of course, I'll never know,
    if idly I sit by.
When time is used talents to grow,
    the talents are not shy.

Time, talent, both are bosom friends;
    they're loyal to the end.
Where one begins the other ends.
    strength each to each will lend.

21. FROM EVENING TO MORN

From evening to morn, the first day,
    so reads a creation account,
a pattern by which we convey
    the twenty-four hours that we count.

The opposites evening and morn,
    with darkness contrasting the light,
may make us be happy or mourn;
    may calm us or may us affright.

Though sadness may come in the night,
    with morning, there may well come joy.
At evening often glows moonlight,
    with morning, sunlight we enjoy.

How different the day and hours
    from minutes we spend in the night,
and often we don't use our powers
    to judge and to do what is right.

From one to hour twenty-four,
    the cycle each day we repeat.
Do we assume there will be more?
    Beware, for death hours will delete.

22. FAMILY TIME

We talk about the weather and
    we chat about our kids.
Sometimes we sit, sometimes we stand;
    no subject one forbids.

It's simply best of family time
    with fathers, mothers, sons,
with daughters small, some in their prime,
    and many little ones.

There are young married folks as well,
    who share parental thoughts,
and others who have tales to tell;
    no one a tale boycotts.

At dinner time the little ones
    share grace before the meal;
the youngest daughters, youngest sons
    make grace indeed seem real.

When families gather nothing can
    surpass togetherness;
they bond as one their lives to span
    in grief or happiness.

23. Making Family Music

My family is musical,
but sometimes it is whimsical,
   which makes me very glad.
From opera to fine art songs
and late-night family sing-alongs
    quite rarely am I sad.

Caruso's glorious tenor voice
was certainly my father's choice.
    One record that we played,
"Celeste Aida" was its name,
had brought Caruso lasting fame,
    a thrilling serenade.

I could not speak Italian then,
but played it over and again
    to hear the glorious sounds.
I savored every thrilling tone
as to another world I'd flown
    beyond all earthly bounds.

My father's baritone was smooth;
his voice was rich with tones that soothe.
    My mother thrilled us too.
The way she made pianos speak
with Chopin or Schumann mystique
    oft won a prized review.

When I discovered I could sing,
it was a most obliging thing,
    for both my sisters played.
They played piano's what I mean;
like mother both their gifts were keen,
    accompanists homemade.

My older sister's played for me
both here and far across the sea,
    and CDs we have made.
My younger sister I adore;
once I was stuck in Singapore,
    and she came to my aid.

From far Alaska's shivering clime
to Singapore, arrived in time,
    there to accompany me.
We had a laugh at her warm clothes,
in Singapore not a soul froze;
    she earned a shopping spree.

Guess what? I also have a son
with whom I have had so much fun.
    He plays piano too.
We've concertized, recorded too,
his son's guitar's now joined our crew.
    I wonder who's in queue.

Though I've sung opera, sung songs
around the world before great throngs,
    the place I'd rather be,
is making family music ring,
the way we oft at Christmas sing
    around the Christmas tree.

24. TODAY WILL SOON BE YESTERDAY

Today will soon be yesterday,
    so nature's cycle goes.
Tomorrow will be yesterday
    much quicker than one knows.

If each today were yesterday,
    would I do what I did?
As I look back at just the way
    some wrong I thought I'd hid?

But yesterday I can't undo,
    unsay what I have said.
I must admit I am the you,
    from whom you asked for bread.

Instead I turned the other way.
    Will I do this again?
Tomorrow will be yesterday;
    can I not break this chain

of looking back from day to day
    with yesterday regret?
Can I learn kindness to convey
    and mercy not forget?

To make today a yesterday,
    a day of no regret—
let kindness always show the way;
    this no one will forget.

25. WHAT A DAY!

You walk down streets of cobblestones;
then stop, a bakery has fresh scones.
You have a taste and drink some tea.
What a delight as friends you see.
You have a chat on this and that;
you leave, but you forget your hat.
You walk on just a block or two,
then suddenly it dawns on you:
your hat you left there on a chair.
This was quite clear with windblown hair.
So back you go to fetch your hat,
and there it is, right where you'd sat.
You put it on, go on your way,
the wind to face, then come what may.

26. Then and Now

If then meets now, will I know how
    this wonder has occurred?
When what is now becomes akin
    to what some thought interred.
Do present and the past relate
    to one another on their own?
Is this uncommon, is this fate,
    is neither one alone?

Søren Kierkegaard, "Life can only be understood backwards,
but it must be lived forwards."

27. BACKWARD—FORWARD

If life is backwards understood
    but forward must be lived,
then let's look back for our own good,
    lest we should be deceived.

Let's learn the lessons from our past
    that guide our future best,
a backward look can life recast
    and redirect each quest.

If backward vision we should lose,
    past lessons will be gone,
from every future path we choose
    experience is withdrawn!

Look backward, life to understand
    and to ourselves be true.
Look forward, our thoughts to expand,
    and new thoughts will break through.

28. A Future from Our Past

In ancient cultures, ancient worlds
 and many-a varied tongue,
are tales in ancient scrolls unfurled,
 some tales by ancients sung.

Enchanting stories of the past
 are keys to who we are;
to each of them we should hold fast,
 each precious, known memoir.

They tell us of our acts and thoughts,
 rehearse our worst mistakes,
when our good will is tied in knots
 and temper overtakes.

Yet, there are tales of our best times
 when we cared for the poor.
We helped those victimized by crimes,
 gave meaning to *amour*.

But what of worlds that we know not,
 the worlds of outer space—
are good and evil there yet known
 and have they left a trace?

Let us these new worlds shape for good
 from what we learned before,
from ancient stories where we've stood
 for truth, for goodness swore?

The future need not past repeat
 but use the best we've learned,
so, hope and goodness both will meet:
 evil with good returned.

Section 3

What Do You Think of What You Think?

29. To Think

There is so little time to think
    of all that one should think about.
And yet from thoughts one dare not shrink,
    lest one be left with only doubt.

It's true, one's thoughts may lead to doubt,
    and selfish thoughts may lead nowhere,
resulting in a mindless rout
    of all except oneself left there.

To think is an auspicious gift
    to everyone in humankind.
Don't let your thoughts then go adrift,
    but nurture them within your mind.

30. The Power of Thoughts

What raises thoughts today to heights
    of meaning everyone should know?
Perhaps if they broach human rights,
    they'll shatter thoughts of old Jim Crow?

If universal meaning be,
    such as, "to your own self be true,"
think not, my friend, the choice is free;
    such thoughts apply to me and you.

Of other thoughts we're free to choose,
    if we have courage them to own.
If not, integrity we'll lose.
    Think not that one can stand alone.

Think how to deal with climate change
    and cures for illnesses that kill,
or education to arrange
    for training in an unknown skill.

Our thoughts have power to create
    a different world in which to live.
Yet, progress they can obviate
    when we refuse them power to give.

31. The Wonder of Thoughts

The night was short without much sleep,
    my thoughts were mixed but clear.
At times it seemed they plunged so deep
    my mind they seemed not near.

There's something wondrous, perhaps fears,
    when thoughts you can't control.
Though happy, you may shed some tears
    that your soul can't be whole.

The splendor of a single thought
    of love, invention, peace,
for ages human minds have wrought.
    I pray this will increase.

32. Sober Thoughts

All prejudice one should oppose,
    for all are due respect.
All hatred human progress slows;
    by hatred lives are wrecked.

Life, liberty, and happiness,
    these rights belong to all,
yet millions know but emptiness,
    democracy's downfall.

33. CONSCIENCE

"Son, let your conscience be your guide,"
    that's what my parents taught.
This daily proverb I have tried,
    but with it I have fought.

One's conscience moral sense assumes—
    to know both right and wrong.
For soundest judgment conscience grooms
    the mind for a life long.

But conscience must be nurtured well
    with wisdom, fairness, truth
by those who all around us dwell
    from childhood through our youth.

The moment that some judgment weighs
    so heavy on our mind,
we know that then our conscience plays
    the role to it assigned.

Its role is this: to help us know
    what we should think or do,
but not in haste; judgment must grow.
    Each option first think through.

Would that today we leaders had
    whose conscience was their guide,
who truly knew what's good and bad;
    their conscience then applied.

34. The Senses

Though Helen Keller had no sight,
through Braille she learned to read and write.

And though she also could not hear,
in life's vibrations sounds were clear.

To value senses one must learn
in this we're often taciturn.

We take for granted senses all;
our silence should each one appall.

So, cherish what you see and hear,
with touch and taste have not a fear.

The touch of love, a fond embrace,
there's nothing that can these replace.

When tasting flavors in our food,
we taste the cultures they include.

So, treasure senses every one,
with them each new day is begun.

35. THREE GIFTS

The gifts of memory, reason, skill
may bless or curse the human will.

At birth their promise in us lies,
with hope the promise never dies.

Each day we live is memory's source
of all that steers us on life's course.

If taught to hate and live by greed,
we'll not remember what we need.

We will not think of love and care,
we'll never know the worst to bear.

Will reason save us from despair?
Not if we close our minds to care.

An open mind to hear each cause
alone redeems oneself from flaws.

Flaws in one's reasoning to admit,
mature the mind and keenest wit.

What then of skill that we are given?
Will we by its full growth be driven?

Or will we let it fallow lie,
or wither like a rose and die?

To nurture skills one, two, or three,
gives memory, reason, grounds to be.

To be, exist, the gift fulfill,
fulfill the best of human will.

The careless use of reason, skill
our memory stymies with a chill,

a chill that freezes them in time,
a tragedy and senseless crime.

These gifts then nurture, help them grow:
an open mind the way will show.

36. THE LINK

My mind is active all the day;
　　it hungers just to think.
It's working when I cannot say
　　if there's a missing link,

a missing link between my thought
　　and action that I take;
when I don't act the way I ought
　　but act for my own sake.

So often thoughts invade my mind
　　of unjust acts today,
of prejudice of every kind
　　that takes one's rights away.

But God forbid that I can't see
　　that I must find a way
to link just thoughts with who I'd be,
　　and those thoughts not betray.

37. KNOWLEDGE VERSUS IGNORANCE

To find yourself, for yourself think,
    said Socrates, the sage.
From your own thoughts you must not shrink,
    your thoughts let come of age.

In knowledge you will find there's good,
    in ignorance there's none.
In knowledge you'll learn what you should,
    and find that good you've won.

The good in knowledge to be found
    is goodness to be shared.
Though ignorance may still abound,
    choose knowledge, uncompared.

38. LEARN KINDNESS

What lies within your own control?
  Your thoughts and what you do?
Take care yourself not to extol,
  lest this be a miscue.

Real self-control's a treasured prize
  among all humankind,
but wars and conflicts emphasize
  that humans can be blind,

be blind to their own faults and greed
  beyond their own control.
They sacrifice what others need;
  they're selfish, that's their goal.

Suppress the hungry, poor, and weak
  and profit from such deeds,
creates a world that's cruel, bleak,
  which soon to discord leads.

How can we selfishness unlearn
  and think of others first,
and generosity discern,
  in caring acts be versed?

Just start with one kind, generous deed,
  a meal for a lone child.
You'll find that you have sown the seed
  of kindness, for she smiled.

39. Kindness, A Frame of Mind

If indolent rich have but scorn
    for needy and the poor,
who're often destitute, forlorn,
    how can their help be sure?

Will someone show their loving care
    for those who need it most:
with food to eat and clothes to wear,
    those who're not self-engrossed?

I saw a man just yesterday
    do what I've never done;
take off his coat, and kneel to pray,
    and give it to someone.

This person only wore a shirt,
    though it was very cold.
This act of kindness I'll assert—
    moved me to be so bold.

When you are kind, you have the power
    to help someone be kind.
The kindness you on others shower,
    it is a frame of mind.

40. Fortune

"Fortune sides with those who dare,"
    said Virgil, Roman sage.
Does it side with those who care,
    with poor folk age to age?

Fortune does not smile on those,
    those who are down and out;
and sharing wealth some oppose,
    for sharing makes them doubt.

They hesitate wealth to share,
    they think, "To share's no good.
What about my own self-care?
    I'm acting as I should."

But those, who will freely give
    of that which is their own
to the poor that they may live,
    transform their hearts of stone.

41. REALITY 1

What are sheep with no shepherd?
    What are shepherds with no sheep?
If spotless were a leopard,
    has one's reason gone to sleep?

What if what we think is not
    the way things are known to be,
Is reality then fraught
    with that which we do not see?

Hard, cold facts, oft hard to find,
    sometimes are before our eyes.
Don't speculate, don't be blind;
    it's best facts not to despise.

Section 4

What Do You Think Really Matters?

42. Peace and Quiet

For peace and quiet there's a price
    which everyone must pay.
What would you offer as advice,
    the options each should weigh?

Should we deny what we believe
    just for the sake of peace?
Will quiet thereby we achieve
    and from all stress release?

Experience will we deny
    which shows us how to live?
If so, no matter how we try,
    this peace will not forgive.

43. Arrogance

When envy's born of arrogance,
    it cripples heart and mind,
and it would surely be by chance
    humility to find.

When arrogance and excess pride
    pervade demeanor, speech,
and civil conscience we deride,
    humility can't teach.

It's time ourselves humbly to ask:
    Will we ourselves revere
and hide behind our ego mask
    so self cannot appear?

44. Pessimism?

Expect what you should not expect
    and disappointment reigns supreme:
when you the best of things reject
    and turn the best to worst extreme.

Expect the best and hope will guide
    your acts, emotions, and your thought.
Then pessimism cannot hide
    behind "to hope is all for naught."

Is not such optimism vague,
    a shallow, Pollyanna view,
that our perceptions oft may plague
    as superficial thoughts accrue?

So, you must then put to the test
    the expectation: hope on hope,
for all that is the very best
    with pessimism's sure to cope.

45. Ambiguity 1

If something is ambiguous,
   its meaning's not exact,
no meaning's then contiguous;
   you're left with the abstract.

The abstract, an idea or state,
   you cannot concretize.
It may be open to debate,
   rarely to compromise.

Ambiguous may be for good,
   or it may be for bad.
If so, do you think that I should
   with what it means be glad?

46. AMBIGUITY 2

Can there be ambiguity
    in morals or in truth,
or do we lack acuity,
    and simply play the sleuth?

If there is no congruity
    in what we say and do,
leave we all to fortuity
    not knowing what is true?

Let's hope there's ingenuity
    if only in a few,
to hold for perpetuity
    what history proves true.

47. Reality 2

Reality has its own will,
 which suits not all who wish to dream,
and fantasy is wont to fill
 our minds with things not as they seem.

If fantasy and dreams are lost
 amid what shapes reality,
then it exacts a drastic cost,
 although our every thought is free.

Nevertheless, reality
 all human beings surely need,
so they'll reject all falsity,
 deception, lying, graft, and greed.

48. DAILY GREETINGS

"Good night, Good morning," oft we say,
kind words of greeting used each day.
But how we say them matters most,
at home, with friends, from coast to coast.
Just add two words, others will glean
something different that you mean.
Good night, my love, dear one, my friend.
Good morning, sweetheart, boy-, girlfriend.
Endearing words can change the way
that others hear what you may say.
Just add a word or maybe two
and see what greeting comes to you.

49. Sadness and Joy

Fear not the sadness of the day,
for sorrows surely pass away.
You cannot know the thrill of joy,
if darkness should your hope destroy.
It may not be with swift release,
but without sorrows there's no peace.
Though joys and sorrows come along
and may be linked to right or wrong,
they are a part of human fate
and come too early or too late.
Both joy and sorrow are good friends;
where one begins the other ends.
When sorrows come, you may then find
rejoicing is not far behind.

50. WHAT MATTERS

What will decide questions of life?
  The way that we view death?
Perhaps the way that we view strife,
  with every living breath?

If morbidly we see our days:
  confined, with no way out,
or simply that each hour delays
  our death and fosters doubt.

If thus we see our destiny:
  each day we death await,
then all is triviality,
  and doom alone our fate.

If all our talents we ignore
  and mark till death the time,
life will be empty, nothing more,
  at death we're in our prime!

51. Life and Love

If life extends and love expends,
    one never lives in vain,
for life intends, always depends
    on love our lives to reign.

Though life is brief, love brings relief,
    and comforts those who live,
for love's the source, the vibrant force,
    which can our faults forgive.

52. Life and Death

Before our death, we first must die,
    there's illness and decay;
these forces for our health will vie,
    they will not go away.

Our health is limited by death,
    disease by some is fought.
Before we take our final breath
    all kinds of cures are sought.

Should we not face the glaring truth,
    death is a part of life?
We all are mortal from our youth,
    not strange our body's strife!

When lying on our beds of pain
    awaiting time to die,
the church comes not to heal, restrain,
    or suffering to belie.

It comes to bring us love and light
    which we in Christ may see,
for suffering gives an inner sight
    into eternity.

The mysteries of eternal joy
    on earth this heaven we know,
when love's the whole of life's employ.
    Christ came such love to show.

His sacrament of love now joins
    this world and that to come.
Nothing we face in life purloins
    the truth, though strange to some.

53. POETRY

Some days there's poetry alive
    in everything I see:
a stone, a word, a lone beehive,
    a giant tulip tree.

They cannot know I see in them
    such simple poetry,
nor when I see in them a gem
    of pleasant symmetry.

For poetry so oft depends
    on phrasing that's not weak.
Of grammar's best it makes good friends,
    and syntax not antique.

There's poetry one least expects
    where words are not in use.
A poem of words, one hopes, reflects
    insight, not its abuse.

54. I Cannot Be Human Alone

I cannot be human alone,
humanity's history has shown
connection to others must be
like friendship between you and me.
Humanity cannot condone
to be human and be alone.
That I am I and you are you
exists because we have the view
that I'm not I and you're not you,
if we are looking for a clue
that isolates us from the rest
of human beings in a quest
to be just who we are alone.
How sad, as history has shown.

55. Humility

The virtue of humility
    had I, I would not know.
It fosters no ability
    humility to show.

Humility is void of pride,
    humility is meek.
Though selfishness it can't abide,
    this does not mean it's weak.

Humility you cannot see,
    except personified.
If one asks, "Is it seen in me?"
    This shows an inner pride.

Humility cannot be known,
    acknowledged in one's mind;
humility yet can be shown
    but cannot be refined.

Those who are humble do not know
    that they may humble be,
for pride can wield a death-knell blow
    to true humility.

56. Hopeless?

Where goodness triumphs, hate subsides;
where goodness triumphs, good abides.
But goodness some folks will reject,
their own self-interest to protect.
No kindness do they others show,
no kind deeds do they seem to know.
With hatred they reject all those
who dress themselves in ethnic clothes,
who speak a language they don't know,
and prejudice they can't let go.
How sad that color of one's skin,
is where much hatred does begin.
Why must some folks so selfish be
and say, "If folks are not like me
and do not think the way I do,
there's no way they can know what's true"?
Without concern and without care
of others' needs to be aware,
there's little hope, and hope is gone
when *different* folks are put upon.

57. Goodness

How can one goodness measure
    when often it's unseen?
How can one goodness treasure
    and know what it may mean?

Is it an exclamation?
    "My goodness," can't you see!
Can goodness be a virtue
    like one's humility?

If goodness is a virtue
    that all should own, possess,
then goodness will not hurt you
    and kindness will express.

Some people think they've got it,
    while others not at all.
But some simply forgot it,
    while others good recall.

Section 5

What Do You Think Makes You Smile?

58. An Octogenarian Viewpoint

I'm eighty-five and I can laugh,
    and that's the solid truth.
It seems that each day's got some gaff,
    so what! I'm not a youth.
So I'll just play along this way
    till all the gaffs are gone,
and laugh until that fated day
    we all must wait upon.

59. Blue

The color blue means many things;
you're blue, you're subject to mood swings.
You're blue, you feel quite down and out.
You're blue, depressed, without a doubt.
You're blue, can mean you're tipsy, drunk.
You're blue does not mean you've got spunk.
Still I like blue, just color blue.
Of colors it's my fav'rite hue.

60. Cobblestones

The cobblestones laid on this street
    were put in place with utmost care.
Their corners don't exactly meet,
    but that's their charm as they lie there.

When cars roll by, they make a sound
    unlike you hear on paved highways.
The rumbles as the tires go 'round
    produce some rhythms that amaze.

I like to walk on cobblestones
    but take great care in snow or rain,
for I could slip and break some bones,
    which would result in undue pain.

Some have a space so large between
    I easily could stub my toe,
and I would know where I had been.
    On cobblestones, I must go slow.

Some cobblestones are red and gray,
    and some are smooth from years of wear.
Some rough ones were always that way,
    a perfect cobblestone is rare.

61. Forget / Remember

Forgetfulness, a daunting thing,
when I should be remembering.

If I forget that I forgot,
it's not that I remembered not.

Not to remember to forget
is different from remember yet.

If I remember and forget,
it's mem'ry's jest and not a threat.

Some things I hope that I forgot
are in my memory, though a jot.

Forget, forgot, remember yet,
I hope that I will not forget.

62. Mama's Blouse

As sheets of rain cover the panes
    of windows through the house,
oh my! It rains, and rains, and rains!
    The clothesline! Mama's blouse!

It will be soaked, what will I do?
    I promised her I'd watch
the weather, yes, the rain clouds too,
    but, oh my! What a botch!

Oh, if the sun would just come out
    and dry out all that's wet,
I'd be relieved without a doubt,
    and mother would not fret.

63. MELODRAMA

Dare melodrama truly last?
It seizes present and the past.
And often mockery it makes;
sincerity it glibly fakes.
Yet, melodrama actuates
imagination and orates.
Sometimes we must admit it's fun
to see how far ideas may run.
Though supercilious be a grin,
it fast reveals just where we've been:
a fact was stretched with heightened flare,
as if the truth could have been there.
Exaggeration is the king;
sensation is the only thing!
Yes, melodrama lives and dies
by many long-extended sighs.

64. Ole Jack

This summer my strawberry roan
    will graze upon the field
outside the barn that he has known
    till his hind leg is healed.

While hitching him up to a plough,
    he jolted, pulled away,
then somehow fell, I don't know how,
    and on the plough blade lay.

The blood flowed quickly to the ground;
    we had to call the vet,
who sewed the gash; the wound was bound,
    the crisis had been met.

A boy of six, I did not know
    how long the wound would heal,
but weeks on end Jack's gait was slow,
    the pain he felt was real.

Ole Jack, we called him by that name,
    possessed a steel-like will.
There was no way his will to maim,
    so he is with us still.

65. QUE SERA SERA?

Better angels of your nature
    do you call on each day?
Do you make with fate a wager
    to keep evil away?

Is there a special talisman
    you've had since you were young,
from an old chief, a salishan,*
    which 'round your neck you've hung?

Have you another lucky charm
    to ward off all that's bad;
will it, you think, keep you from harm,
    so that you're never sad?

I doubt that *que sera sera***
    is really what you think.
And you will shout a loud "Hurrah!"
    to find a missing link.

A talisman, a lucky charm,
    protects or haunts your thoughts,
but destiny you can't disarm
    by casting mental lots.

* A name referring to a member of a group of American Indian peoples inhabiting areas of the northwestern US and the west coast of Canada.

** Whatever will be, will be.

66. TEA TIME FOR LEO AND LOU

A field mouse called Leo by name
    lived near an old farm house's well.
Each time that the farm owner came
    to draw water Leo would yell.

He'd yell, "Sister, you must look out!
    or you will be wet through and through.
The farmer's bucket's leaking spout
    could ruin our small house of bamboo."

Right by the well the field-mouse house
    was standing tiny as can be,
and Leo and his sister mouse
    were just about prepared for tea.

But water from the bucket's spout
    filled up their tea room to the brim,
and Leo thought, "I'll work this out,
    the situation's not so grim."

Their door he opened with a jerk;
    the water rushed right out the door,
Just then he thought his plan would work:
    two cups of water, nothing more,

he'd catch it before all was gone.
    Yes, just enough for tea for two,
so tea time they could carry on—
    for Leo and his sister Lou!

67. THE SUGAR CANE TRUST

My summers as a boy were fun;
    I visited Aunt Jane,
who always wished for her own son
    to harvest sugar cane.

She owned a giant farm down south
    where she grew sugar cane,
and stories told by word of mouth
    of her were never plain.

I loved the way she walked and spoke,
    I hung on every word.
She'd tell a tale, end with a joke,
    and nothing was absurd.

One morning when my chores were done,
    she took me by the hand,
and said, "The fun has just begun.
    You'll see what I have planned."

"Where are we going to go, Aunt Jane?"
    I asked. We walked along.
And then I smelled cut sugar cane
    and knew I wasn't wrong.

"Aunt Jane, we're headed for the mill,"
    I yelled and jumped for joy,
and then I saw it! What a thrill!
    She said, "You'll load, my boy!"

There was Ole Sol, her faithful mule,
    who turned the grinder 'round.
Aunt Jane then said, "Let Ole Sol cool,"
    as I stood by spellbound.

As cane was brought in from the road,
  Aunt Jane then said to me,
"This year the grinder you will load.
  You're old enough, you'll see."

It is a dangerous task, indeed,
  for you could lose a hand.
"Be careful as the cane you feed,"
  was Aunt Jane's loud command.

That was the first day I felt grown;
  I felt like a young man!
Aunt Jane such trust in me had shown.
  That was her master plan.

"Get ready with the cane," she said,
  "It's time to start Ole Sol."
The grinder turned and then I fed
  the cane; I did it all!

Aunt Jane stood by and smiled at me.
  I dared not smile at her,
but concentrated so she'd see
  one could not me deter.

Aunt Jane had put her trust in me
  as years and summers passed,
and I, with utmost certainty,
  learned trust endures, will last.

Oh yes, one thing from my Aunt Jane
  you really need to know:
"You must taste some sweet sugar cane.
  Its sweetness makes you glow!"

68. Moonlit Railroad Tracks

I walked along some railroad tracks,
as evening moonlight made them glow
like endless trails of shooting stars,
as far as I could see.
For miles, it seemed far down the tracks
a parallel design of lights
would sparkle on the long, straight rails
as waving tree limbs hovered there
by the light of the full moon.
Then all at once the wind made sounds
I thought were from a xylophone,
for there before my eyes it seemed
the cross ties were its keys.
It's amazing what you can imagine
with moonlit railroad tracks!

69. THIS OR THAT

If *this* or *that* means either-or;
one should know what the choice is for.
Perhaps there's not a choice at all,
just *this* is large and *that* is small.
If you are faced with such a choice,
it's best to have an active voice.
For someone may say, "I'll take *that*,"
and you'll stand there holding your hat.

70. TWO STYLES

The *Jugendstil* that's on this street
    is unlike *Georgian* on the next.
When architects came there to meet,
    were they all pleased, or just perplexed?
Or did one architect decide—
    on parallel streets of this town:
"I'll put the two styles side by side,
    monotony I will strike down"?

Perhaps these houses years apart
    were built solely by owner's taste,
the visual appeal of art
    on which the various styles are based.
Perhaps one liked art nouveau style,
    the other neo-classical.
One looks and wonders all the while
    that side by side they're magical!

71. You

What difference does it make,
    if you are who you are?
If you're you, not a fake,
    you're better off by far.

It's better to be you
    than what another thinks,
but do you have a clue,
    or is this self-high jinks?

If you think that you know
    the who it is you are,
is this the you, you show,
    or is it your memoir?

The memoir of the you
    you really thought you were,
but never thought it through,
    so, you are just a blur.

If this is not the case,
    then you are really fine.
Your you, you need not chase,
    just say, "My you is mine."

72. Uncle Lane's Sugar Cane

Last fall when all the fields were green
    with ripened sugar cane,
the prettiest I have ever seen
    were fields of Uncle Lane.

The vast and broad, extended fields,
    a harvest-ready scene,
bring hope of profitable yields
    that Uncle Lane might glean.

I love to ride the little train
    that brings in all the cane,
in warmth of sun or in the rain,
    again and once again.

The little engine chugs along;
    its wood-fired engine strains,
then shows that it is very strong,
    as Uncle Lane explains:

"When all the open cars are full,
    their weight can be a ton;
the little engine strains to pull
    its load till work is done."

Now I am old enough to drive,
    and I'm the engineer.
How great it is to be alive,
    the train engine to steer!

I haul in loads of sugar cane
    so sugar can be made.
The profits made by Uncle Lane
    we'll toast with lemonade.

73. Grandma and Grandpa's House

I walked along a mountain ridge,
then crossed the valley on a bridge,
that leads to grandma Anna's home,
and also my grandpa Jerome.
They lived right on the mountain edge
behind a giant rock-formed ledge.
I loved to stand there, gaze for miles
when autumn leaves in colored styles
showed off their beauty all around,
the valley with rich colors crowned.
The front porch was a pleasant place
where grandpa reigned like king of Thrace.*
And grandma always was my queen,
hers was a pleasant, smiling mien.
When grandpa, grandma passed away,
their will gave me the right to stay
my life long in their mountain home,
my thanks to Anna and Jerome.

* Thrace is a geographical and historical region in southeastern Europe encompassing parts of today's Bulgaria, Greece, and Turkey.

74. POOR MUMFORD

A chipmunk jumped out of the grass
when Jane's white Persian saw it pass.
The cat, named Mumford, lunged at it,
but then the chipmunk showed its grit.
A race began like lightning's flash,
and then I heard a giant crash.
The chipmunk disappeared, I thought,
as Mumford's tail was trapped and caught.
It yanked it loose but tipped a bin
of garbage and I had to grin.
The clattering noise scared the chipmunk
as it dashed off, it showed its spunk.
The race was over, Mumford stood
alone in his own neighborhood.

Section 6

What Do You Think of Love?

75. WHAT IS LOVE?

Like the North Star, love is there.
Love's a guide with sincere care.
Love is constant, wavers not,
love alone is love's own lot.
Love's a beacon, brilliant light,
guiding lovers, day and night.
Though one's weak, love's always strong;
true love's faithful all life long.
True love lives and never dies.
True love thrives and never lies.
When there's discord, love unites.
Love seeks healing, avoids fights.
What a treasure love to taste;
such a treasure's not to waste.
Love can sense and love can feel
heart-born love that's always real.
Love is ageless, with us still,
love is life's own greatest thrill.

76. A Thought of Love

A momentary thought of love,
　　reflection of the tenderest kind,
enthralls the spirit, soars above
　　all mediocre thoughts of mind.

One moment of such love in time
　　surpasses every trivial thought;
it needs no poetry or rhyme.
　　Sublime, that it one's spirit caught.

77. CHILD LOVE

A little child cannot know
that someone may love it so,
unless warm arms it embrace
with love that one can't replace.
With soft kisses on the cheek
a child's future is not bleak.
Your love it senses when there;
it knows when your love you share.
For love all children are made
but not for love's masquerade.
Give love to a child in turn,
and love to you will return.

78. Family Love

Though you are far away just now,
    our hearts are aching for you near;
the distance will all hearts endow
    with strengthened love till you are here.

Your absence will in us renew
    the family love that will not wane.
The bond we share each one goes through
    and binds us in all joy and pain.

Each one strength from the other draws,
    on one another all depend.
Such love endures without a pause,
    for parent, child, and every friend.

79. In Love

In love two bodies form one soul;
in love two bodies form a whole.
In love the other one comes first;
in love there is an endless thirst.
In love one thirsts true love to show;
in love one casts aside ego.
In love your lover is your friend;
in love that's true there is no end.
In love, sealed often with a kiss,
is love, true love's ethereal bliss.
In love, in love one's whole life long,
in love is heaven, myst'ry, song.

80. Love and Trust

One's love at all times trust requires,
    for love evolves each day.
Evolving love never retires
    when trust is its mainstay.

To trust another's love sustains
    the spirit and the soul.
Through trust enduring love remains,
    for trust seeks no control.

Return we shall, all dust to dust,
    whether or not we love.
But love that's soundly based on trust
    is like a peace-borne dove.

81. LOVE

Love creates, willingly transforms;
   love bridges a divide.
Love soars to heights above all norms;
   no feelings can it hide.

Love is a leveler, a plane
   that smooths emotion flares.
It does not cover up or strain
   the depth of earnest cares.

Love strengthens those who take the chance
   to love someone and trust.
Trust makes of love a real romance,
   care for one's love, a must.

82. Love's Abode

What does it mean, love's in the heart,
    or love is in the mind?
Keeps every sinew, every part
    in you so intertwined,
that who you are and want to be
    on shared love now depends,
and your eternal, lasting plea:
    "I pray it never ends."

83. More Than Life

When windblown flowers wave and bend,
and autumn leaves their colors lend,
when lovers touch them hand in hand,
and kiss as in some distant land,
no bliss can match these tender scenes,
nor can one say what each one means.
One only senses in the heart,
the gift of love's mysterious art.

84. Oh, For a Love Like Yours!

The moon shines brightly, I can't sleep;
I close my eyes with thoughts so deep
   and hope that slumber comes.
I hear no sound; it is quite still;
my body won't obey my will.
   My inner spirit hums.

The tune it hums is the first song
I sang when I knew we belong
   together for always.
I sang it then, I sing it now,
ev'n if I at your grave must bow.
   I'll sing it all my days.

What fortune God brought you my way;
what fortune you with me did stay
   with love that never died.
The beauty of your lovely eyes,
your honest love that bore no guise,
   your love you did not hide.

If I should live a hundred years,
your love my every day endears
   until eternity.
I only hope my love for you,
like yours, will me each day renew.
   This love is ecstasy!

85. Singing Eyes

Within your eyes there is a song,
a melody, ever so strong.
The sound endures and does not die;
it makes my spirit laugh and cry.
The glorious melody takes wings,
makes me forget all other things.
This song comes from your soul, I knew
the time your eyes first came in view.
How is it that one's eyes can sing,
and you hear not another thing?
I did not know then what I heard:
a love song—now I know each word.

86. The Greatest Power

Love is at times a fickle thing
that moves the heart like flowers in spring.
Love can at times make the heart glad,
at others makes the heart feel sad.
But love can be a constant thing,
the source of life and its wellspring.
In constancy love cares for all
and lifts all those who tend to fall.
In constancy love cares for one
for whom in love all will be done.
Love is the greatest power on earth,
a life potential from our birth.
It's ours to choose if love will live;
it's ours to choose if love we'll give.

87. The Joy of Senses

The morning light opens my eyes
to see a world oft in disguise,
and yet a world to make me wise.

The eyes may filter right from wrong,
assess life's beauty all day long,
inspire the lips and heart with song.

To touch my loved one's tender hand,
caress her face without demand,
and sense she loves me, oh how grand!

To hear the words, "I love you, dear,"
are sounds that help me deep to peer
into her soul and sense her near.

The joy that comes with each embrace,
no sorrow ever can efface,
for love leaves an eternal trace.

88. THEY WELL COMBINE

The words "caress" and "tenderness"
　　one simply can't define.
They're not explained by more or less
　　and yet they well combine.
If you caress with tenderness,
　　you'll find the living art
of love that from the start will bless,
　　for it comes from the heart.

Caresses one should not suppress,
　　and hurried should not be,
but do not use them to impress;
　　they're for sincerity.
And tenderness a lifetime long
　　must captivate your heart,
or your caresses will go wrong
　　and keep your love apart.

89. To Love

To love another gives life worth,
though this one does not know at birth.

A mother, father, sibling love
is something I'm oft thinking of.

But lovers share a special love
that fits just like a hand and glove.

Their love fills up the open heart;
it's there to stay, never to part!

90. The Day Begins

The day begins with thoughts of you,
these thoughts are fresh as morning dew.
These thoughts in me quickly awake
the depths of love that me remake,
remake, remold me in your love,
your love that is so far above
the heights of all my fondest dreams,
enriched by such enchanting themes
that you personify, make real:
your tenderness that makes me feel
your gentleness I can't resist,
and so I ask, "Does love exist?"
And there you are before my eyes,
a gentle glimpse of paradise.

91. RESISTLESS LOVE

Resistless love how can there be?
    I've heard that it exists.
Yet many will perhaps agree
    such love one oft resists.
Resistance easily we learn,
    if love does not persuade
someone for our desires to yearn,
    or else we feel betrayed.

Why should one love at all resist,
    if love is the intent?
How can the truth of love persist,
    and one to love consent?
Perhaps one knows, or one knows not
    when genuine love one finds.
Most certainly, it can't be bought;
    it's found in hearts and minds.

What does it mean, love's in the heart,
    or love is in the mind?
Keeps every sinew, every part
    in you so intertwined,
that who you are and want to be
    on shared love now depends.
Then in your mind you've but one plea:
    "I pray it never ends."

Bibliography

Arendt, Hannah. *The Life of the Mind: The Groundbreaking Investigation on How We Think*. New York: Harcourt Brace Jovanovich, 1978.

Ariely, Dan. *Predictably Irrational: The Hidden Forces That Shape Our Decisions*. New York: HarperCollins, 2008; 2nd edition, 2012.

Descartes, René. *Discourse on the Method of Rightly Conducting One's Reason and of Seeking Truth in the Sciences*. 1637.

Grant, Adam. *Think Again. The Power of Knowing What You Don't Know*. New York: Penguin, 2021.

Haidt, Jonathan. *The Righteous Mind. Why Good People Are Divided by Politics and Religion*. Pantheon, 2012.

Heidegger, Martin. *Discourse on Thinking*. New York: Harper Torchbooks, 1959.

————. *Off the Beaten Track*, trans. by Julian Young and Kenneth Haynes. Cambridge: Cambridge University Press, 2002. The German title is *Holzwege*.

————. *Poetry, Language, Thought*, trans. by Albert Hofstadter. New York, Harper & Row, 1971.

Hobbes, Thomas. *Leviathan, or the Matter, Form, and Power of a Commonwealth, Ecclesiastical and Civil*. Collier Classics in the History of Thought. New York: Collier Books, Collier MacMillan Publishers, 1962, 43–44.

Hunter, David A. *A Practical Guide to Critical Thinking*. Wiley. Ebook, 2013.

Jacobs, Alan. *How to Think: A Survival Guide for a World at Odds*. New York: Currency, 2017.

Kahneman, Daniel. *Thinking Fast and Slow*. New York: Farrar, Straus, and Giroux, 2011.

Lakoff, George and Mark Johnson. *Metaphors We Live By*. Chicago: University of Chicago Press, 2003.

Lawrence, Jerome and Robert E. Lee, *Inherit the Wind*. London: English Theatre Guild, Ltd., 1961.

Lewis, C. S. "'Bulverism' or, The Foundation of Twentieth Century Thought," in *God in the Dock*. Essays on Theology and Ethics. Grand Rapids: Eerdmans, 1970, 271–77.

Ricouer, Paul. *Interpretation Theory: Discourse and the Surplus of Meaning*. Fort Worth, TX: The Texas University Christian Press, 1976, esp. 5.

Scruton, Roger. *The Uses of Pessimism*. New York: Oxford University Press, 2010.